PIANO
Adventures®

Arranged by Nancy and Randall Faber

A BASIC PIANO METHOD

Production: Frank and Gail Hackinson

Production Coordinator: Philip Groeber

Editors: Elizabeth Gutierrez and Edwin McLean

Cover and Illustrations: Terpstra Design, San Francisco

Engraving: Tempo Music Press, Inc.

FABER
PIANO ADVENTURES®

3042 Creek Drive
Ann Arbor, Michigan 48108

Alfred

D1379216

ISBN 978-1-61677-256-7

FIRST NOTES FOR MUSIC READING

This set of notes is used for the first six songs in this collection.

- Play and say the note names aloud as a warm-up for these popular songs.

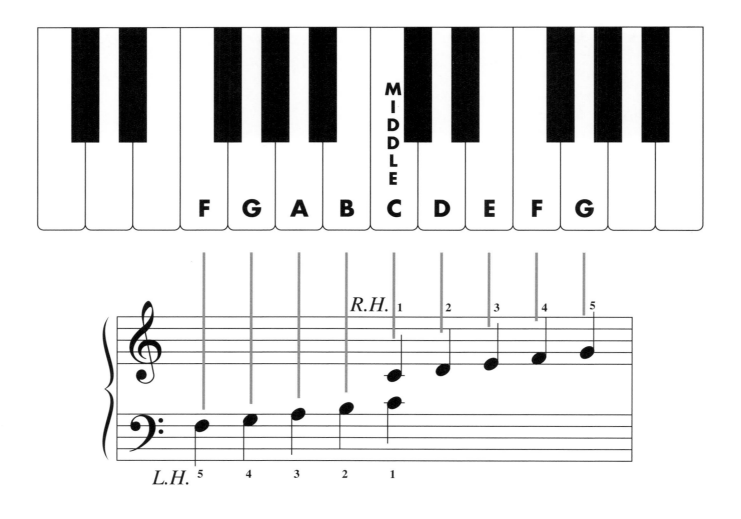

- As your teacher points to a note on the staff, see how quickly you can find and play it on the piano keyboard.

CONTENTS

A **tie** connects two notes on the same line or space.
Hold for the length of both notes combined.

 = 8 beats

Catch a Falling Star

Words and Music by
Paul Vance and Lee Pockriss

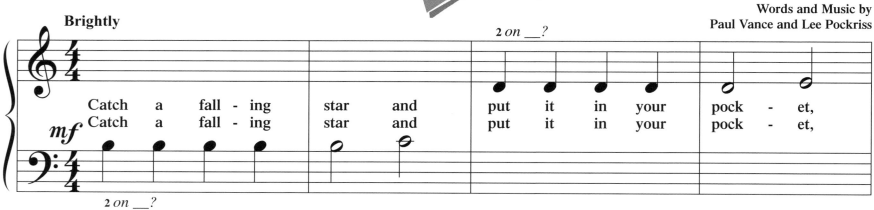

Brightly

2 on __?

2 on __?

Catch a fall - ing star and put it in your pock - et,
Catch a fall - ing star and put it in your pock - et,

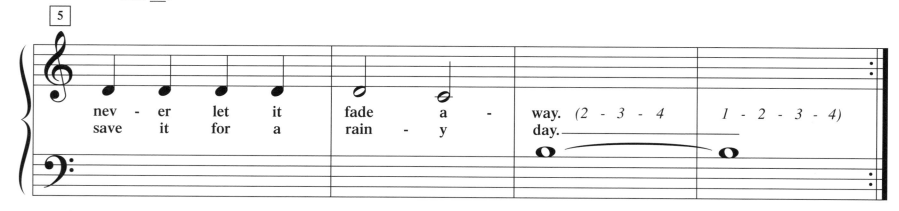

nev - er let it fade a - way. *(2 - 3 - 4* *1 - 2 - 3 - 4)*
save it for a rain - y day.

DISCOVERY **Steps** move from a *line to the next space* or a *space to the next line*.
Point out three measures with steps. Do the notes **step up** or **step down**?

Teacher Duet: (Student plays 1 octave higher)

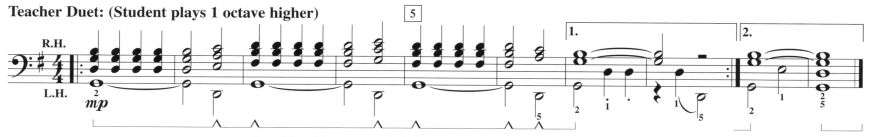

R.H.

L.H.

FF1256

A Starry Ending
"...and never let it fade away"

Create a "starry ending" by playing the last
four measures of *Catch a Falling Star* in higher
octaves, softer and softer. Listen to the sound!

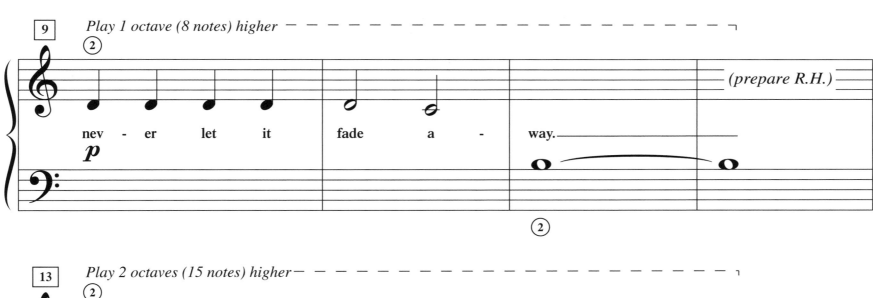

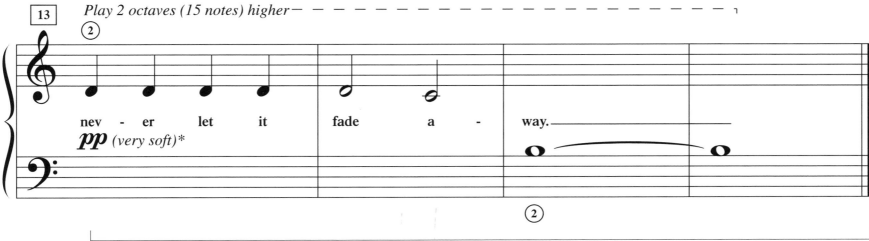

Hold the right-foot (damper) pedal down. *(optional)*

$\boldsymbol{pp}$ - pianissimo (pyah-NEE-see-moh)

This piece begins with an **upbeat** (or pick-up note). The upbeat leads into the first full measure. If a piece has an upbeat, the last measure will often be incomplete. The combined beats of the incomplete first and last measures will equal one full measure.

I'd Like to Teach the World to Sing
(In Perfect Harmony)

Words and Music by
B. Backer, B. Davis, R. Cook, and R. Greenaway

Cheerfully

I'd like to teach the world to sing in per - fect har - mo - ny; I'd
I'd like to see the world for once all stand - ing hand in hand, and

like to hold it in my arms and keep it com - pa - ny.
hear them ech - o through the hills and peace through - out the land.

DISCOVERY **Skips** move from a *line to the next line* or a *space to the next space.*
Circle all the skips in this piece. (Hint: There are 11.)

Teacher Duet: (Student plays 1 octave higher)

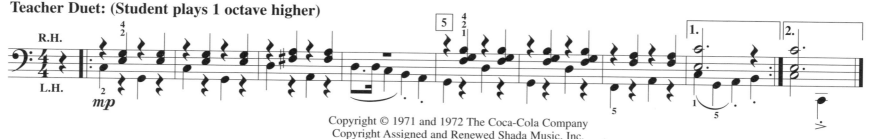

FF1256

"I'd like to hold it in my arms..."

- Connect each child's note to the correct **letter name** on the world below.

- As your teacher points to a child from around the world, see how fast you can play the note.

Extra Credit: Can you number each finger on the hands above?

Happy Birthday to You

Words and Music by
Mildred J. Hill and Patty S. Hill

- Find and circle the **fermata** in this piece.

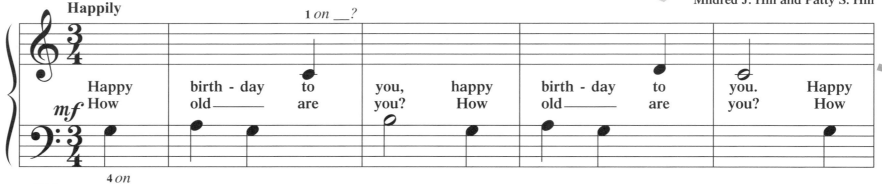

Happily

1 *on* ___?

| Happy | birth - day | to | you, | happy | birth - day | to | you. | Happy |
| How | old ——— | are | you? | How | old ——— | are | you? | How |

mf

4 *on* ___?

5

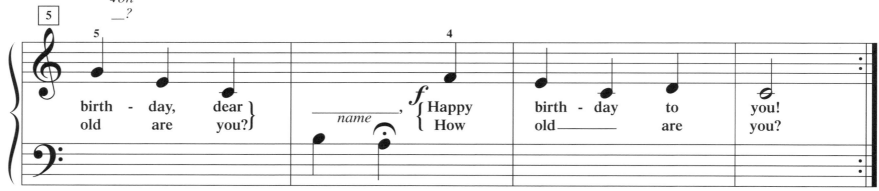

| birth - day, | dear | | | *name* , *f* | Happy | birth - day | to | you! |
| old | are | you? | | | How | old ——— | are | you? |

4

Write your age in tied notes. For example, 9 years old = 𝅝 ‿ 𝅝 ‿ ♩. ⌐ ¬ *your age*

Teacher Duet: (Student plays 1 octave higher)

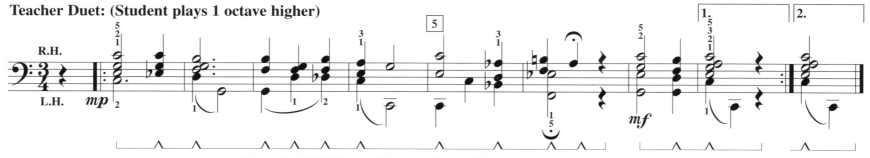

FF1256

Birthday Notes

• Draw a **whole note** on the cake to match the letter name of each candle.

When is *your* birthday? _____

Dynamics means the "louds and softs" of music.

f – forte (pronounced "FOR-tay") means loud

mf – mezzo forte (pronounced "MET-soh")
means moderately (medium) loud

p – piano means soft

Sound Check: Can you play each verse
with the dynamic given?

Lyrics by
Paul Rugg

The Planets
from *ANIMANIACS*

Music by
Richard Stone

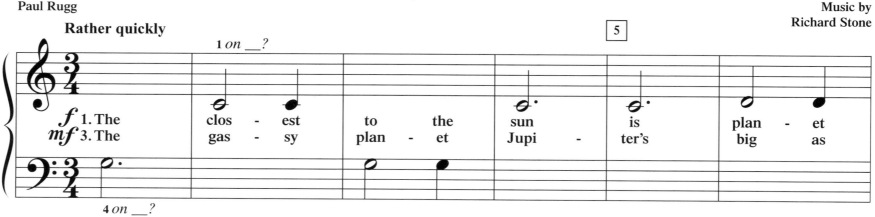

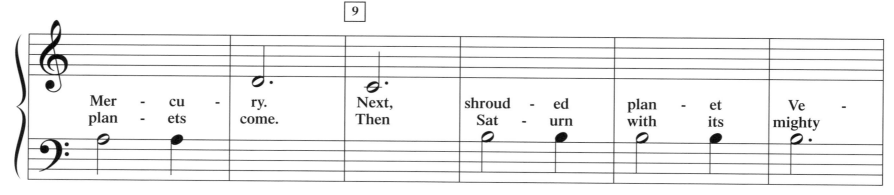

Teacher Duet: (Student plays 1 octave higher)

10

FF1256

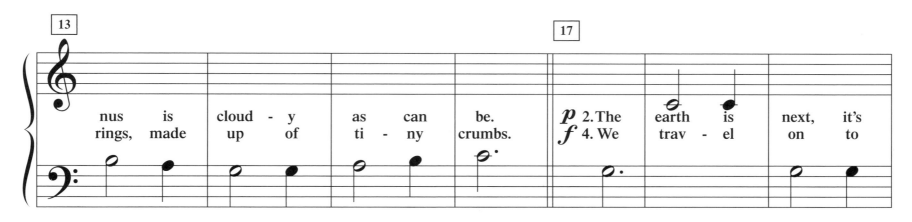

nus is | cloud - y | as can | be. | 2. The | earth is | next, it's
rings, made | up of | ti - ny | crumbs. | 4. We | trav - el | on to

home; | let's | hope it | stays that | way. | And | then there's
Nep - | tune, | gas - sy, | freez - ing | ball. | And | cold and

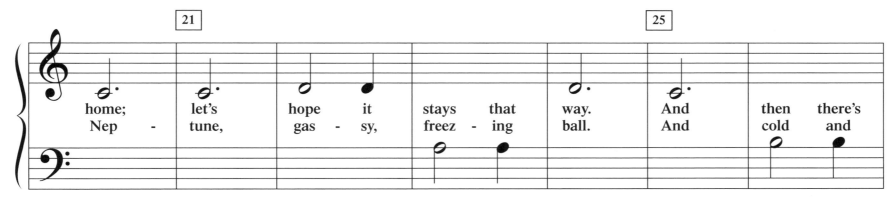

Mars, it's | real | red, oh, | what more | can I | say?
ti - ny | Plu - | to's the | fur - thest | one of | all.

DISCOVERY

Circle all the **repeated notes** in this piece.

- Add bar lines after every **3 beats** to match the time signature.

- Choose your own **dynamic mark** for each verse and write it in the box. Then play using this *new L.H. fingering*.

Mapping the Solar System

The Planets
from *ANIMANIACS*

Music by
Richard Stone

Lyrics by
Paul Rugg

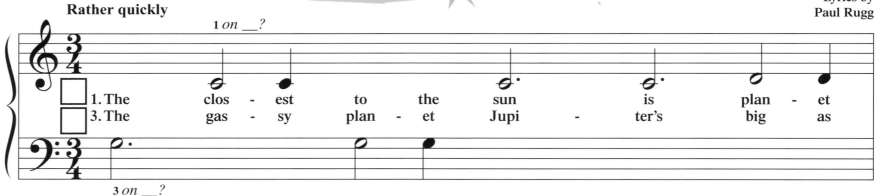

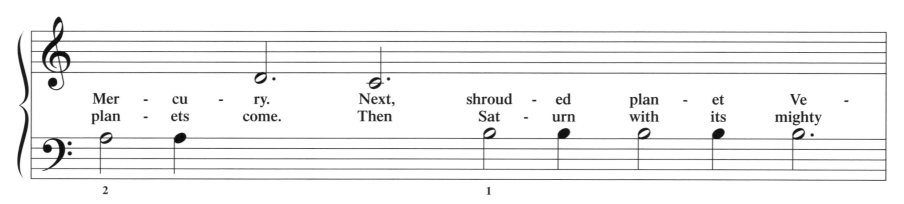

FF1256

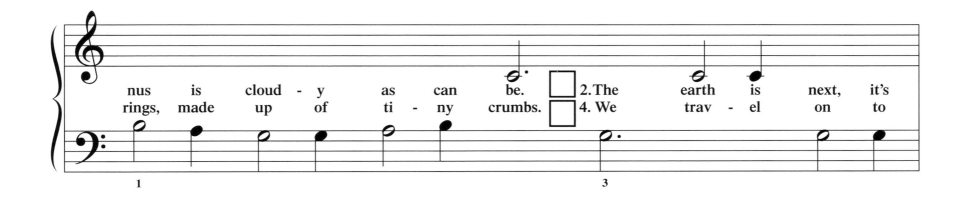

nus is cloud - y as can be. 2. The earth is next, it's
rings, made up of ti - ny crumbs. 4. We trav - el on to

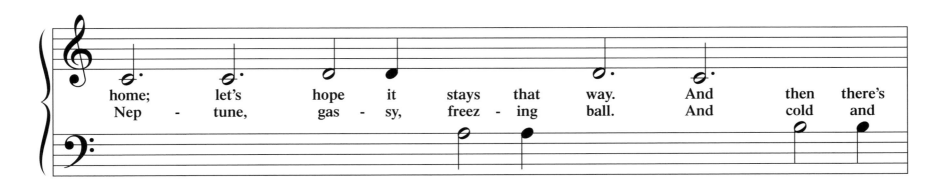

home; let's hope it stays that way. And then there's
Nep - tune, gas - sy, freez - ing ball. And cold and

Mars, it's real red, oh, what more can I say?
ti - ny Plu - to's the fur - thest one of all.

Teacher Note: Tap the opening rhythm and have the student imitate before playing.

Notice the L.H. fingering at *measure 7*. Prepare your L.H. before you begin.

The Lion Sleeps Tonight

New Lyrics and Revised Music by
George David Weiss, Hugo Peretti, and Luigi Creatore

Moderately

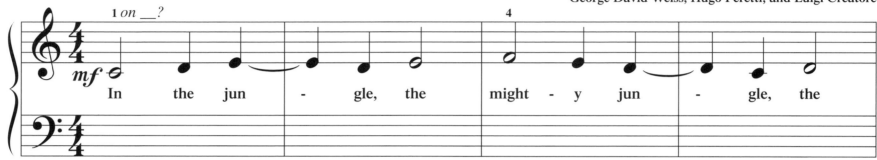

In   the   jun   -   gle,   the   might   -   y   jun   -   gle,   the

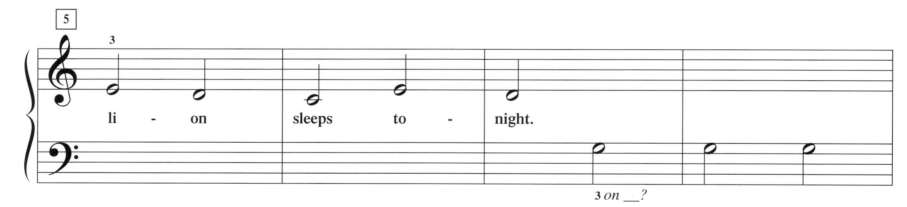

li   -   on   sleeps   to   -   night.

Teacher Duet: (Student plays 1 octave higher)

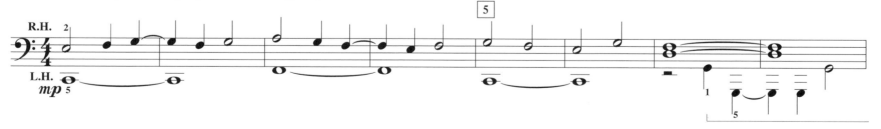

FF1256

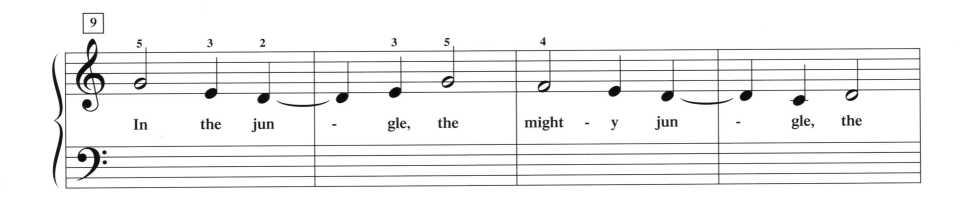

In   the   jun   -   gle,   the   might   -   y   jun   -   gle,   the

li   -   on   sleeps   to   -   night.   p

DISCOVERY The notes of a skip may be played separately or together .
Circle all the skips in this piece. (Hint: There are five.)

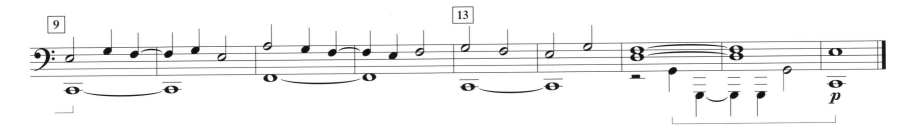

The Lion Sleeps Another Night

This version of *The Lion Sleeps Tonight* begins on a different note and has **missing ties**.

- Add **ties** to match the rhythm of the melody on pages 14-15.
- Name the notes in the blanks. Then play.

The Lion Sleeps Tonight

New Lyrics and Revised Music by
George David Weiss, Hugo Peretti, and Luigi Creatore

Moderately

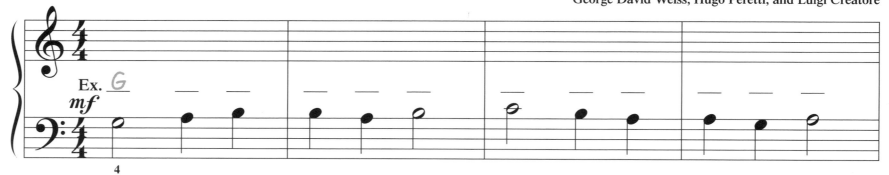

Ex. *G*

mf

4

Teacher Duet: (Student plays 1 octave higher)

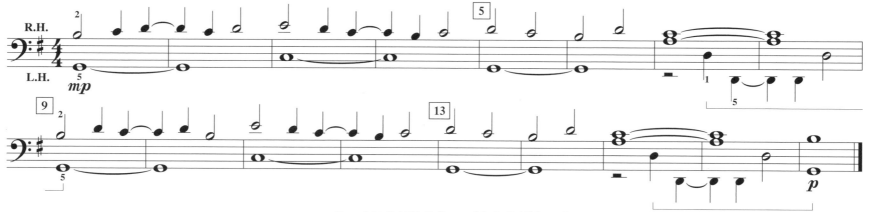

R.H.

L.H. *mp*

5

9   13

p

FF1256

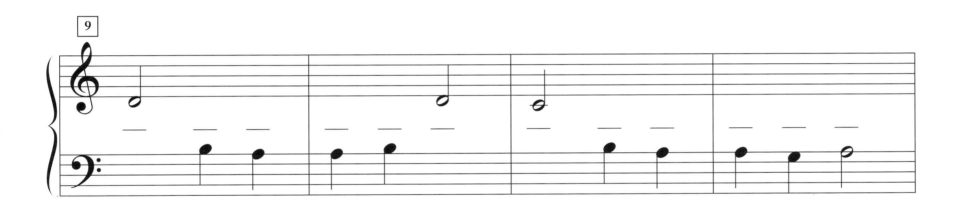

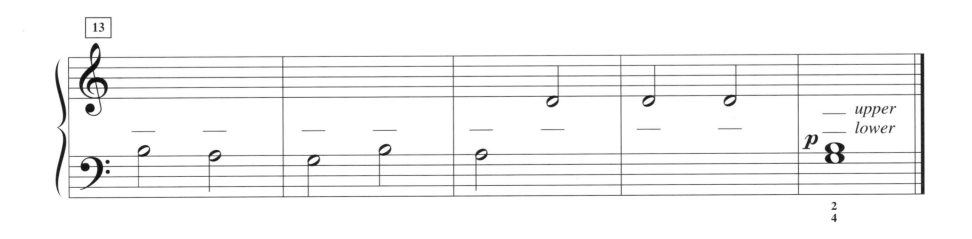

♩ Quarter Rest
1 beat of *silence*.

You write the lyrics!

At *measures 6* and *14*, fill in the blank with something you really like. For example, dog, bike, etc.

I Got Rhythm

Music and Lyrics by
George Gershwin and Ira Gershwin

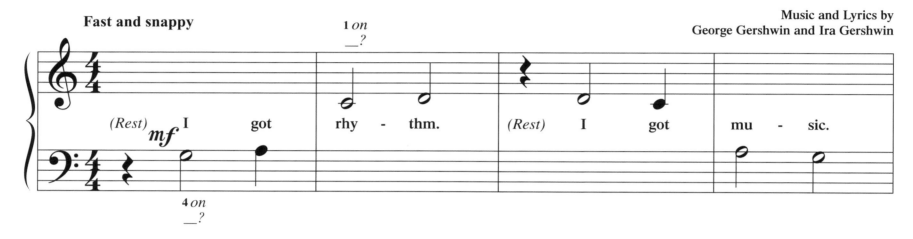

Fast and snappy

1 *on*
___ ?

(Rest) *mf* I got rhy - thm. (Rest) I got mu - sic.

4 *on*
___ ?

Teacher Duet: (Student plays 1 octave higher)

FF1250

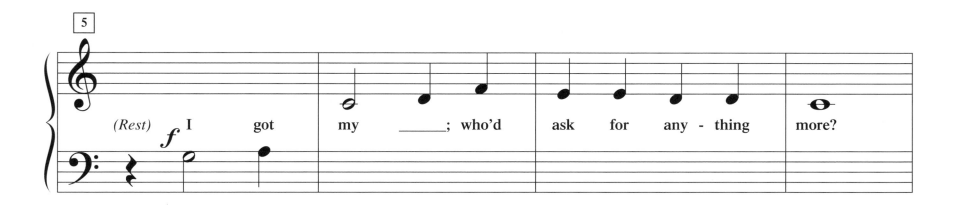

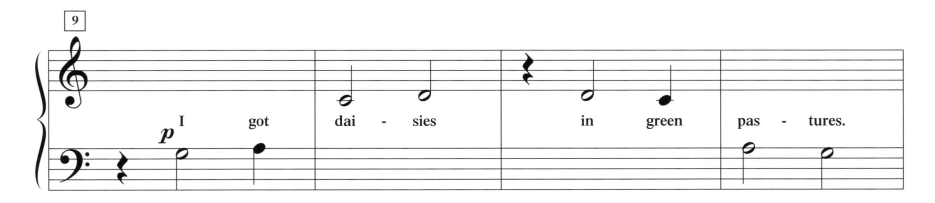

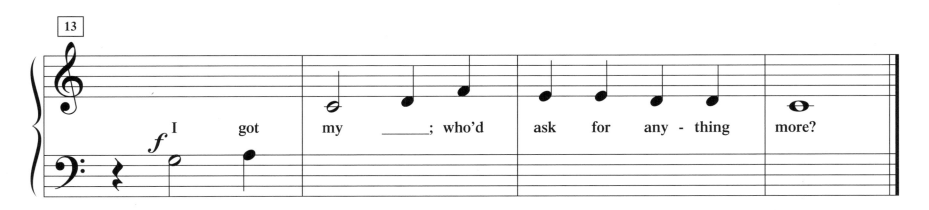

DISCOVERY Your teacher will play *I Got Rhythm* and stop on any note.
Listen carefully and point to the last note played.
(**Teacher Note:** Do this several times.)

I Got More Rhythm
(Rhythm Variation)

Rhythm Award: If you learn to play this piece with perfect rhythm, circle the trophies at the end of the piece.

I Got Rhythm

Music and Lyrics by
George Gershwin and Ira Gershwin

Fast and snappy

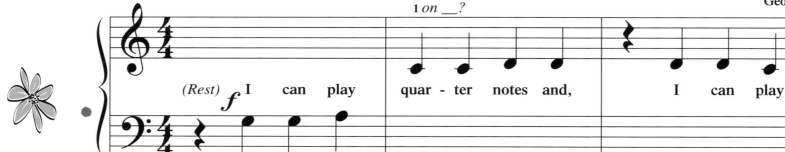

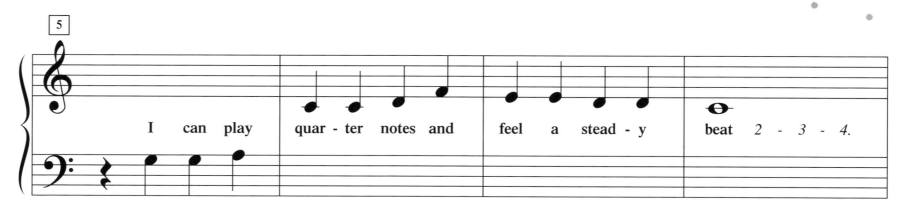

FF1256

9

p I feel a half - note dot and I feel a half - note dot and

13

f I feel the rhy - thm; who could ask for any - thing more?

Three C's

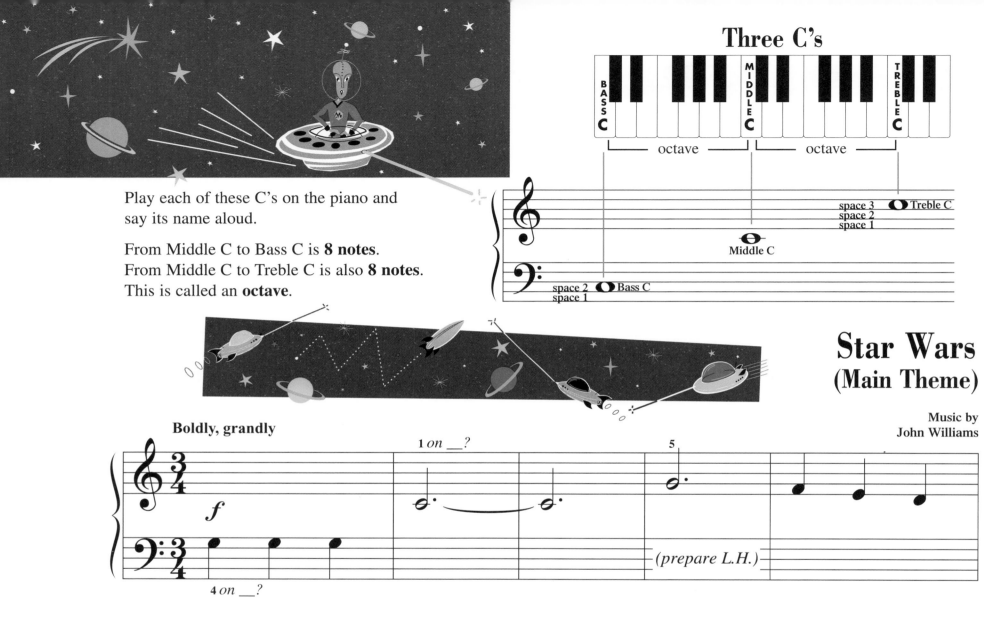

Play each of these C's on the piano and say its name aloud.

From Middle C to Bass C is **8 notes**.
From Middle C to Treble C is also **8 notes**.
This is called an **octave**.

Star Wars
(Main Theme)

Music by
John Williams

Boldly, grandly

1 *on* __?

4 *on* __?

5

(*prepare L.H.*)

Teacher Duet: (Student plays 1 octave higher)

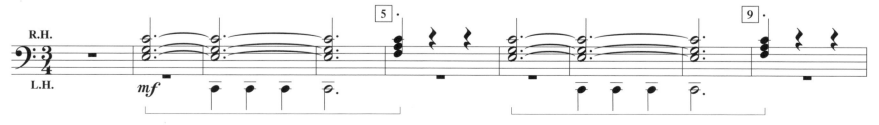

R.H.

L.H.

mf

5

9

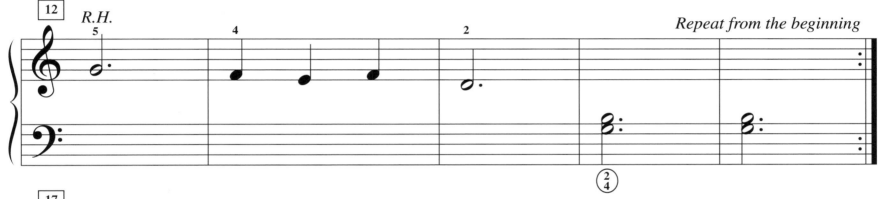

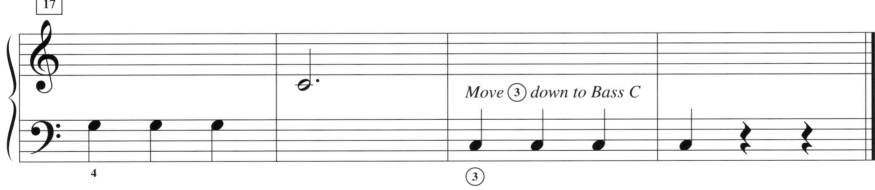

DISCOVERY What is the highest note in this piece? _____ What is the lowest? _____

How many **octaves** apart are these notes? _____

Counting Galactic Melodie[s]

• Write the correct counts for the stars in each melody.

Star Wars
(Main Theme)

Music by
John Williams

1. Write "**1-2-3**" in each measure.

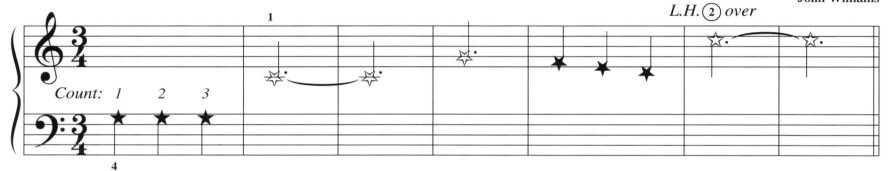

L.H. ② *over*

Count: 1 2 3

Catch a Falling Star

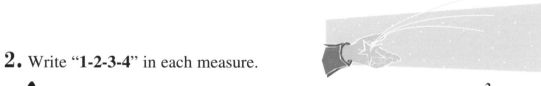

Words and Music by
Paul Vance and Lee Pockriss

2. Write "**1-2-3-4**" in each measure.

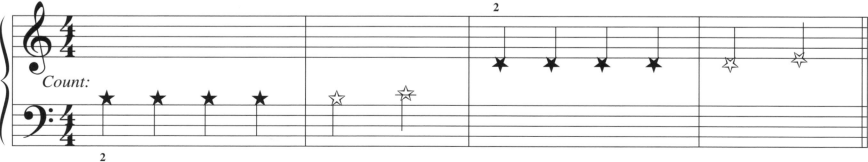

Count:

FF125[1]

The Planets

from ANIMANIACS

3. Write "**1-2-3**" in each measure.

Music by
Richard Stone

Lyrics by
Paul Rugg

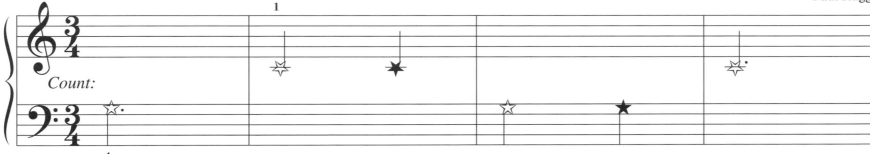

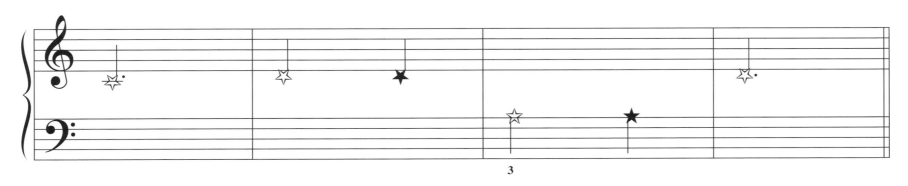

4. Now play each galactic melody, counting aloud "**1-2-3**" for $\frac{3}{4}$ or "**1-2-3-4**" for $\frac{4}{4}$.

Warm-up: Find and play the notes of C Position. Say the note names aloud.

C Position

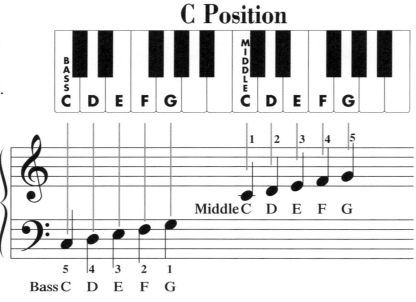

Middle C D E F G

1 2 3 4 5

Bass C D E F G

5 4 3 2 1

Lean On Me

Words and Music by
Bill Withers

Moderately

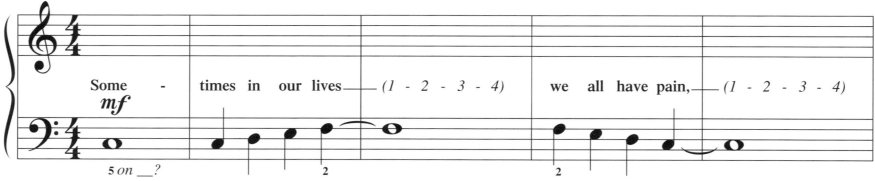

Some - times in our lives___ (1 - 2 - 3 - 4) we all have pain,___ (1 - 2 - 3 - 4)

mf

5 *on* __?   2   2

Teacher Duet: (Student plays 1 octave higher)

R.H.

L.H.

mp

FF1256

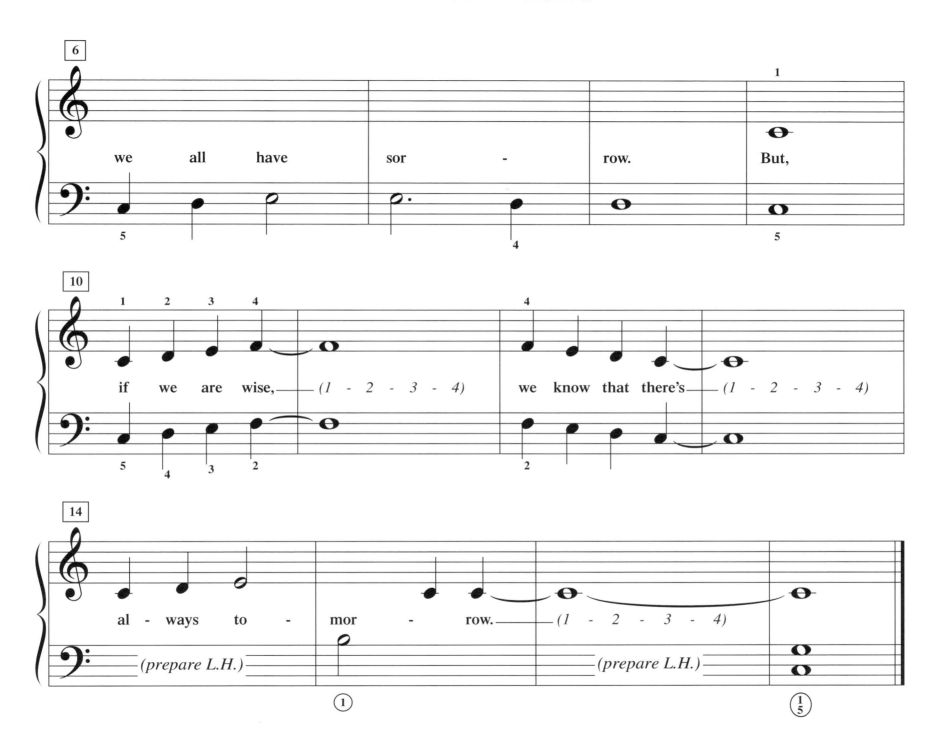

DISCOVERY The ties in this piece always occur on: (*circle one*)

beat 2 to **beat 3**   **beat 3** to **beat 4**   **beat 4** to **beat 1**

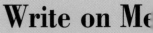

Rules for Stems:

Notes below line 3 have
UP stems on the right side.

For example, **Bass C.**

Bass C
stem up (on the right)

Notes on or above line 3 have
DOWN stems on the left side.

For example, **Bass D, E, F, G.**

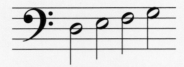

Bass D, E, F, G
stems down (on the left)

Write on Me

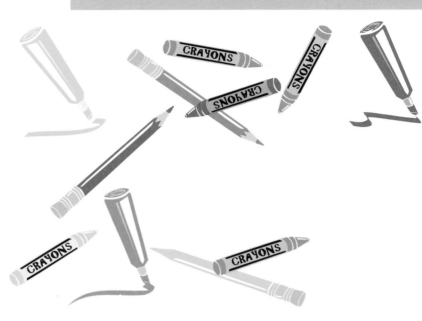

- For each arrow, write the bass clef note an
  octave lower than the treble clef note above.

Review: An **octave** is the distance of 8 notes.
(For example, Middle C to Bass C.)

Lean On Me

Words and Music by
Bill Withers

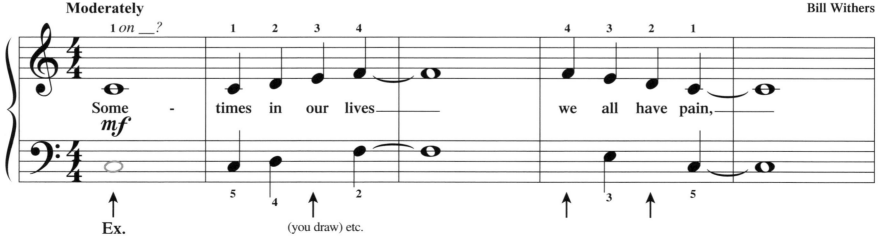

FF125

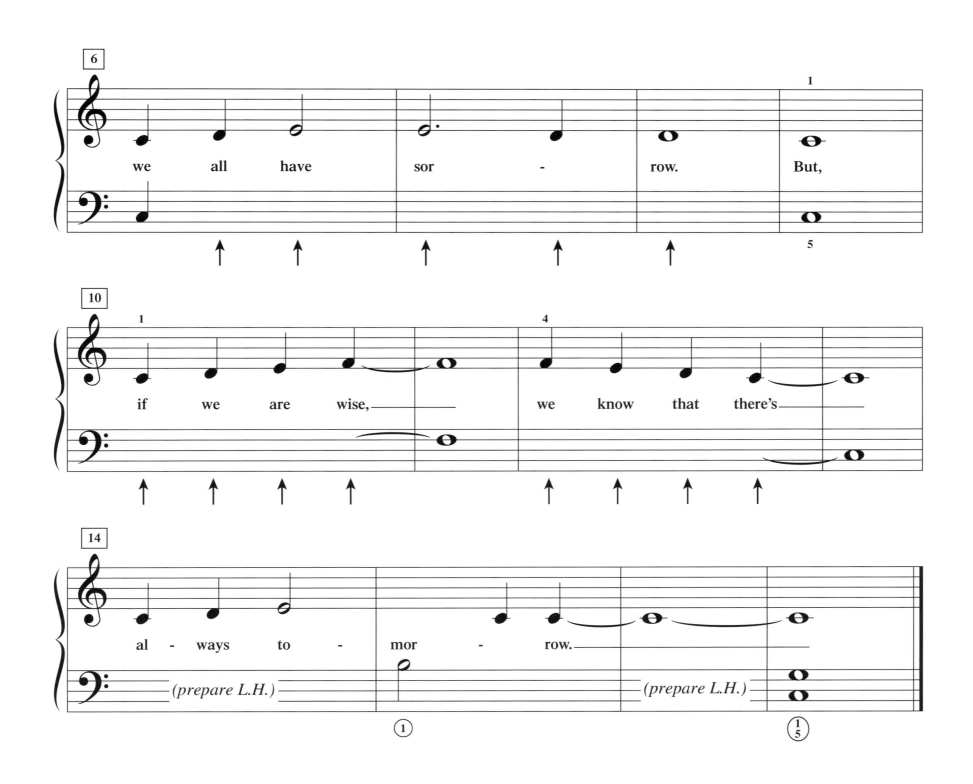

The Rose

Name the position. _____

Words and Music by
Amanda McBroom

Rather slowly

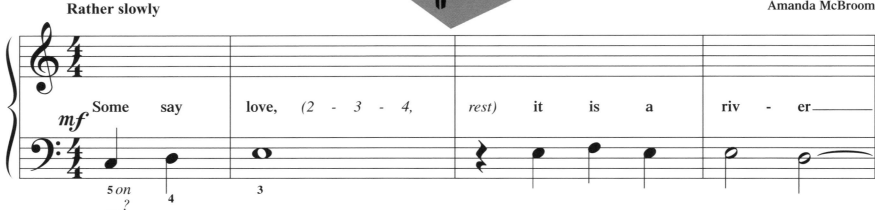

Some say love, (2 - 3 - 4, rest) it is a riv - er

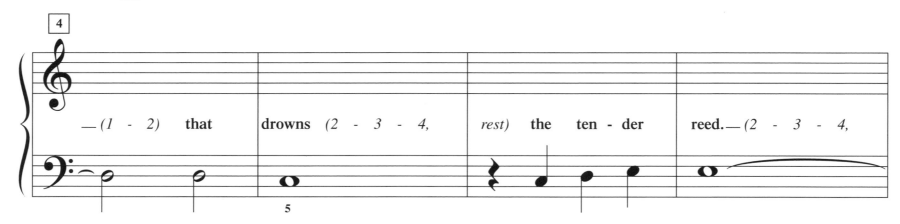

—(1 - 2) that drowns (2 - 3 - 4, rest) the ten - der reed.—(2 - 3 - 4,

Teacher Duet: (Student plays as written, without pedal)

FF12

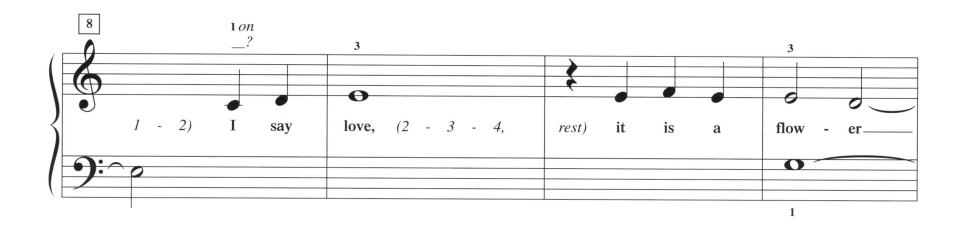

8

1 *on*
—?

1 - 2) I say love, (2 - 3 - 4, rest) it is a flow - er——

12

—(1 - 2) and you (2 - 3 - 4, rest) its on - ly seed.

DISCOVERY

Tell your teacher why the last measure has only 2 beats.

Press the damper pedal down.

12

Musical Roses

- Draw a line from each note on the staff to the rose with the matching letter name. (This page reviews all the notes you have learned in this book.)